TANGOS FOR ACCORDION

Arranged by Gary Meisner

ISBN 978-1-4803-5476-0

HAL•LEONARD®
CORPORATION
7777 W. BLUEMOUND RD. P.O. BOX 13819 MILWAUKEE, WI 53213

Visit Hal Leonard Online at
www.halleonard.com

A MEDIA LUZ
(The Light of Love)

English Lyrics by BORIS RANDOLPH
Spanish Lyrics by ERNESTO FLORES
Music by EMILIO DONATO

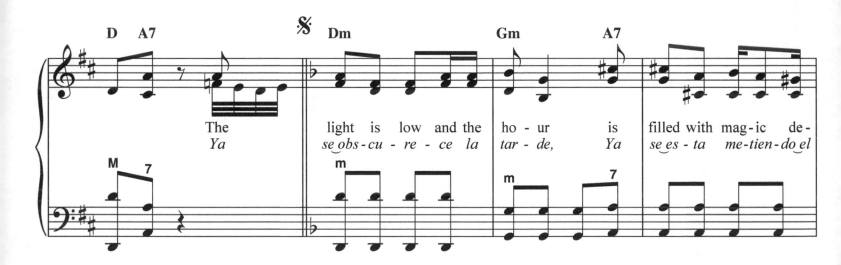

The
Ya

light is low and the
se obs-cu-re-ce la

ho-ur is
tar-de,

filled with mag-ic de-
Ya se es-ta me-tien-do el

light.
sol,

And your hair still holds my
Y tu be-llos o-jos

flow-er,
bri-llan

while your eyes are strange-ly bright. A song from and old re-
con in - ten - so res - plan - dar. *De* *tus la - bios he - chi -*

cord - ing fills the room with one more theme, and
ce - ros *bro - tan pa - la - bras de a - mor,* *pe -*

long-ings that I have treas-ured wake to a tan-go-time dream.
ro cuan - do a - man - tes *be - san* *son cual fue-go a-bra - sa - dor.*

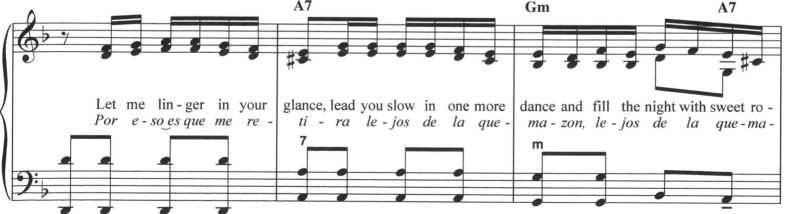

Let me lin-ger in your glance, lead you slow in one more dance and fill the night with sweet ro-
Por e - so es que me re- *ti - ra le - jos de la que-* *ma - zon, le - jos de la que-ma-*

mance. While lights are low, my
zon. Mas cuan-do̱a me - dia

dear, there's ro-mance in the air. My heart is filled with
luz, muy so - li - tos los dos cam-bia-mos las ca -

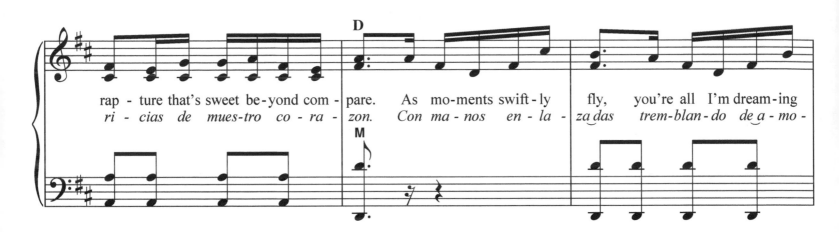

rap - ture that's sweet be-yond com - pare. As mo-ments swift - ly fly, you're all I'm dream-ing
ri - cias de mues-tro co - ra - zon. Con ma - nos en - la - za das trem-blan-do de̱a - mo -

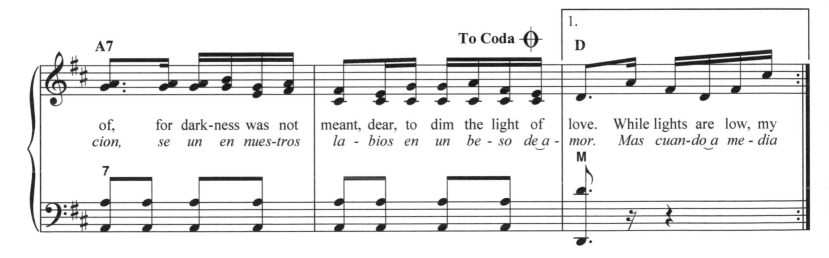

To Coda ⊕   **1.**

of, for dark-ness was not meant, dear, to dim the light of love. While lights are low, my
cion, se un en nues-tros la - bios en un be - so de̱a - mor. Mas cuan-do̱a me - dia

2.

D.S. al Coda
(with repeat)

love.
mor.

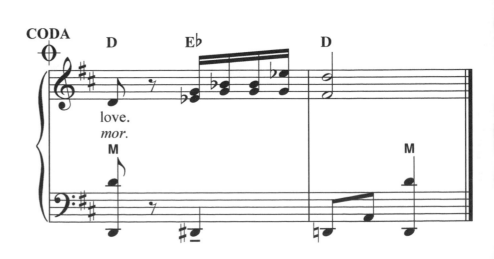

CODA
⊕

love.
mor.

AMAPOLA
(Pretty Little Poppy)

By JOSEPH M. LACALLE
New English Words by ALBERT GAMSE

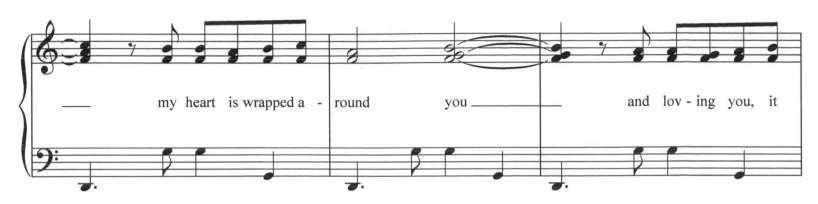

my heart is wrapped a - round you _____ and lov - ing you, it

C　　　　　　　　　C#dim　Dm　　　G7

seems　to　beat　a　rhap-so-dy.　　A - ma -

C

po - la, _____ the pret-ty lit-tle pop - py, _____

A7

must cop-y its en-dear - ing charm from

you. _____ A - ma - po - la, _____

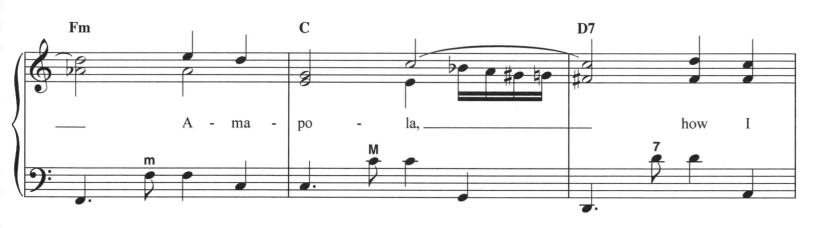

_____ A - ma - po - la, _____ how I

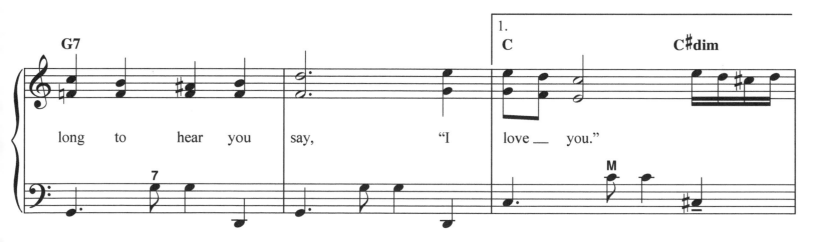

long to hear you say, "I love __ you."

A - ma - love __ you."

AQUELLOS OJOS VERDES
(Green Eyes)

Music by NILO MENENDEZ
Spanish Words by ADOLFO UTRERA
English Words by E. RIVERA and E. WOODS

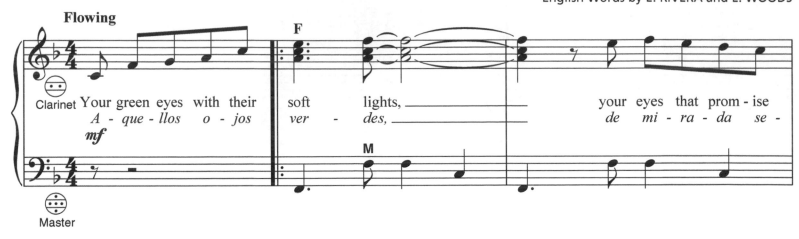

Your green eyes with their soft lights, _____ your eyes that prom-ise
A - que-llos o - jos ver - des, _____ *de mi - ra - da se -*

sweet nights _____ bring to my soul a long - ing _____
re - na _____ *De-ja-ron en mi al - ma*

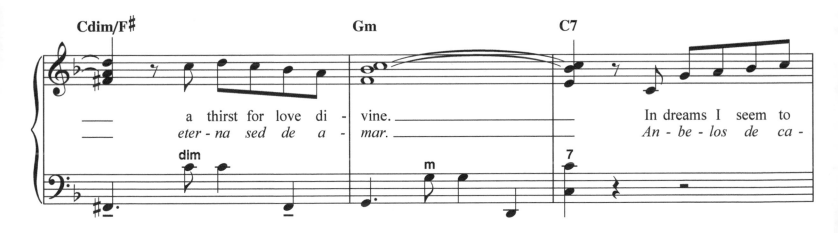

a thirst for love di - vine. _____ In dreams I seem to
eter - na sed de a - mar. _____ *An - be - los de ca -*

hold you _____ to find you and en - fold you _____
ri - cias _____ *de be - sos y ter - nu - rars* _____

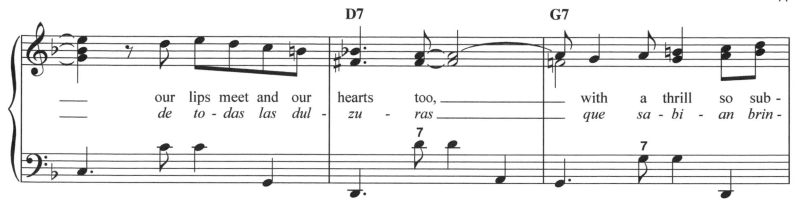

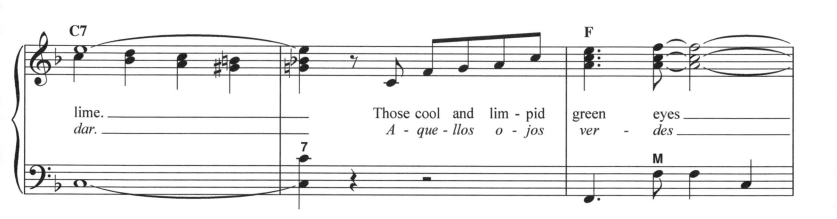

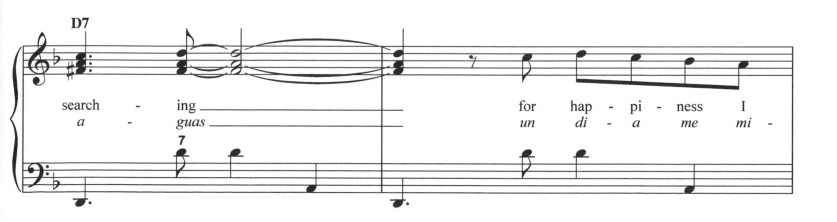

fear. _____
ré. _____

That they will ev - er haunt me _____
No sa - ben las tris - te - zas _____

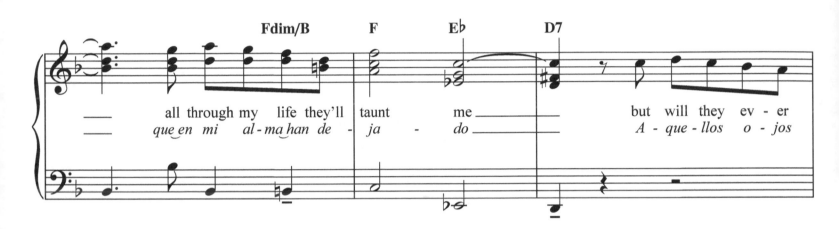

_____ all through my life they'll taunt me _____ but will they ev - er
_____ que en mi al - ma han de - ja - do _____ A - que - llos o - jos

want me _____ green eyes make my dreams come true.
ver - des _____ que yo nun - ca be - sa - ré.

Your green eyes with their true.
A - que - llos o - jos ré.

BLUE TANGO

By LEROY ANDERSON

HERNANDO'S HIDEAWAY
from THE PAJAMA GAME

Words and Music by RICHARD ADLER
and JERRY ROSS

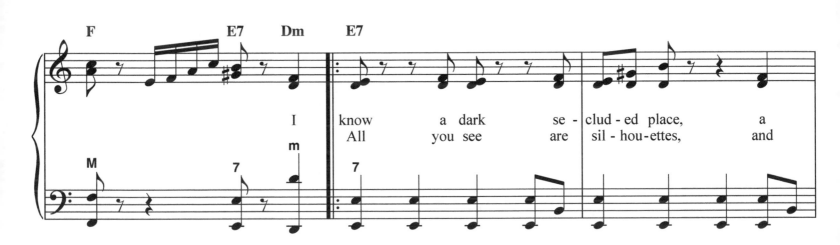

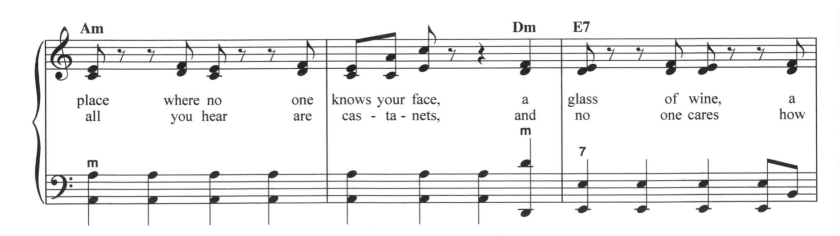

fast em - brace, it's called Her - nan - do's Hide - a -
late it gets, not at Her - nan - do's Hide - a -

1. way! O - lay!

2. way! O - lay! *(Instrumental)*

At the Gold - en Fin - ger - bowl or

an - y place you go, *(Instrumental)*

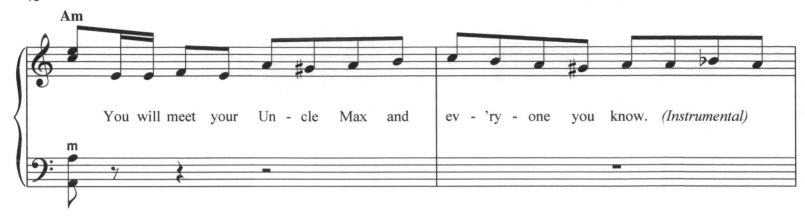

Am

You will meet your Un-cle Max and ev-'ry-one you know. *(Instrumental)*

A7

Dm

But if you go to the spot that

Dm **B7** **Bdim** **B7**

I am think-ing of, You will be free to gaze at me

E7 **E♭7** **E7** **Dm** **E7**

and talk of love! Just knock three times and

I GET IDEAS

English Lyrics by DORCAS COCHRAN
Music by JULIO CESAR SANDERS
Spanish Lyrics by CESAR FELIPE VEDANI

With movement

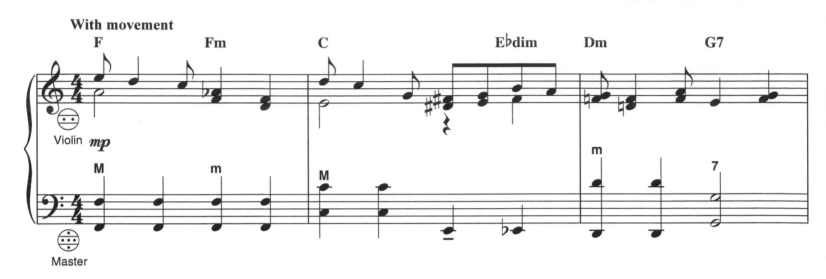

When we are danc-ing and you're dan-ger-ous-ly near me, I get i-

deas,___ I get i-deas.___ I wan-na hold you so much clos-er than I

C   **E7**

too.   Your eyes are al - ways   say - ing   the things you're nev - er

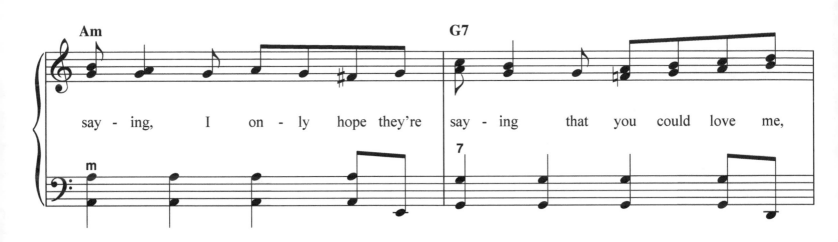

Am   **G7**

say - ing,   I on - ly hope they're   say - ing   that you could love me,

C   **C7**   **F**   **Fm**   **C**   **E♭dim**

too.   For that's the whole i - dea, __ it's true, the   love - ly i - dea __ that I've

Dm   **G7**   **1.** **C**   **G7**   **2.** **C** **G7** **C**

fall - en in love with   you.   When we are   you.

JALOUSIE
(Jealousy)

Spanish Words by BELEN ORTEGA
English Words by VERA BLOOM
Music by JACOB GADE

one but me ____ has won your heart. But, when the mu - sic

starts my peace de - parts. From the

mo - ment they play ____ that lan-guor-ous strain ____

and we sur - ren - der to all ____ its charm once a-

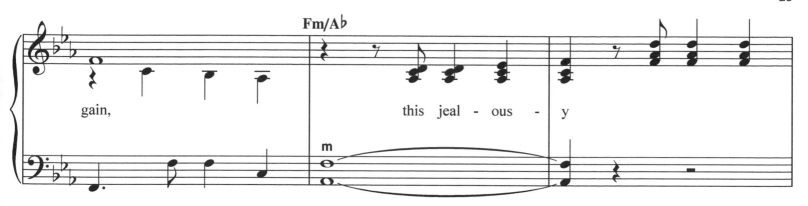

gain, this jeal - ous - y

that tor - tures me is ec - sta - sy,

mys - ter - y, pain! We

dance to a tan - go of love, your

KISS OF FIRE

Words and Music by LESTER ALLEN and ROBERT HILL
(Adapted from A.G. VILLOLDO)

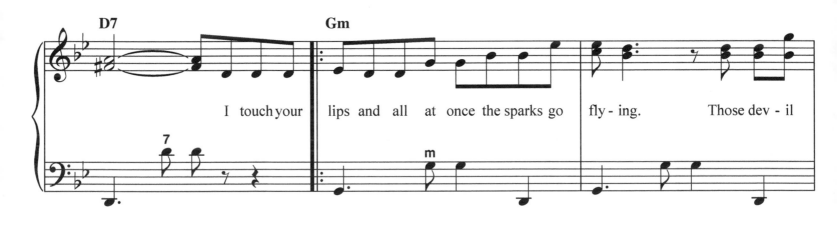

I touch your lips and all at once the sparks go fly - ing. Those dev - il

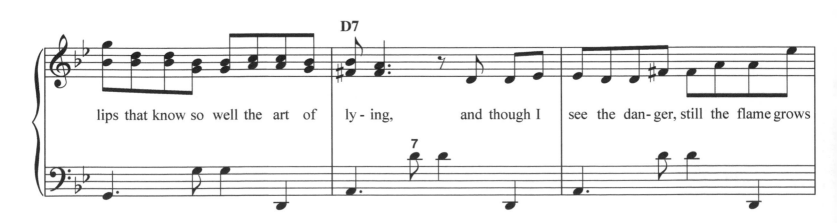

lips that know so well the art of ly - ing, and though I see the dan - ger, still the flame grows

high-er. I know I must sur-ren-der to your kiss of fire. __ Just like a

torch you set the soul with-in me burn-ing. I must go

on a-long this road of no re-turn ing, and though it burns me and it turns me in-to

ash-es, my whole world crash-es with-out your kiss of fire. I can't re-

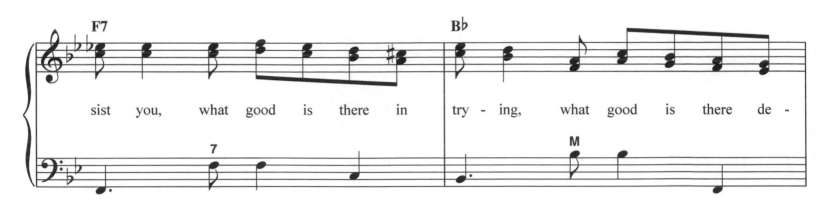

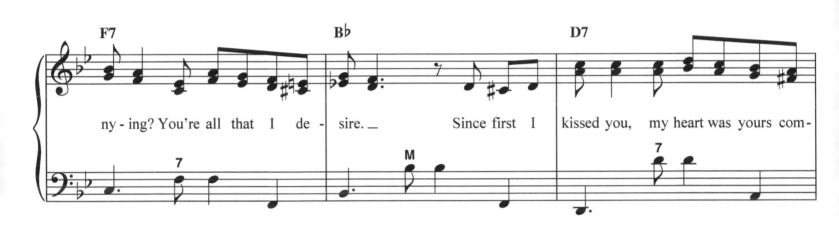

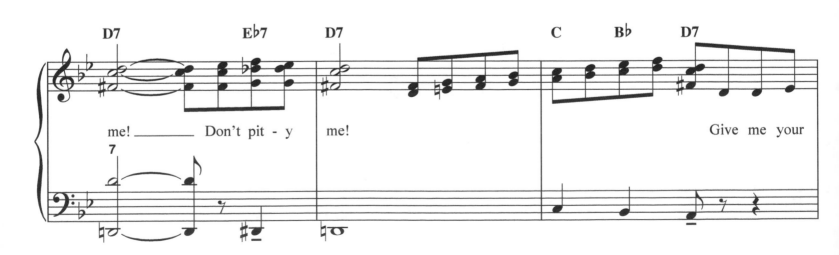

lips, the lips you on-ly let me bor-row. Love me to-night and let the dev-il take to-

mor-row. I know that I must have your kiss al-though it

dooms me, though it con-sumes me your kiss of fire. I touch your

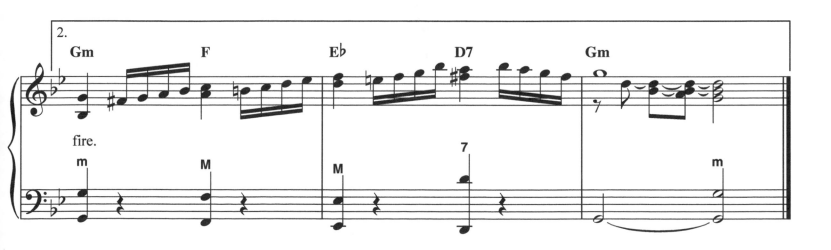

fire.

LA CUMPARSITA
(The Masked One)

Words and Music by GERARDO MATOS RODRIQUEZ,
PASCUAL CONTURSI and ENRIQUE PEDRO MORONI

Love - ly masked one,
Spend with me the

I rec - og - nize you,
dol - o - rous ho - urs,

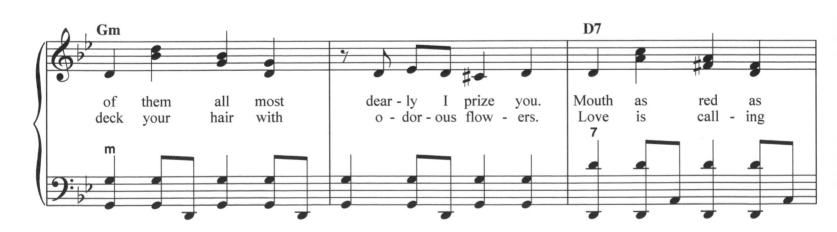

of them all most
deck your hair with

dear - ly I prize you.
o - dor - ous flow - ers.

Mouth as red as
Love is call - ing

Fling a - way your black dis - guise. _____

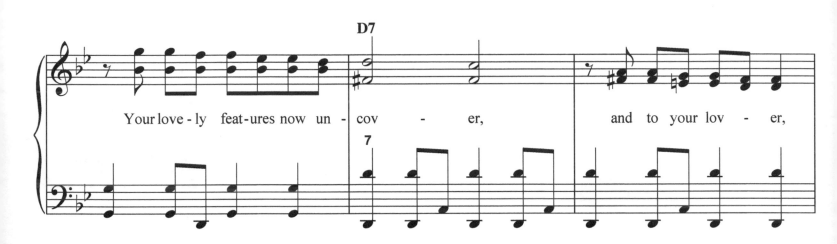

Your love - ly feat-ures now un - cov - er, and to your lov - er,

show your sweet eyes. Come on, beau - ti - ful, oh, come! _____

Pleas-ure waits, and love is call - ing. E - ter - nal voice of des - tin -

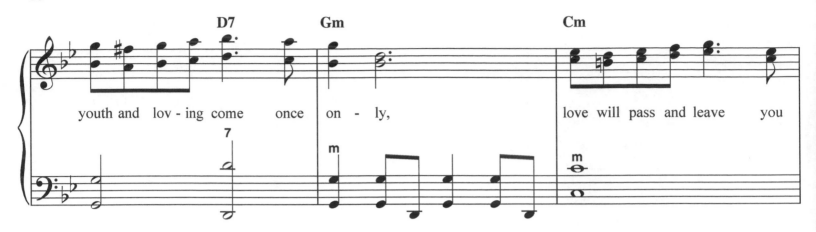

youth and lov - ing come once on - ly, love will pass and leave you

lone - ly. Re - fuse not joy and pleas - ure.

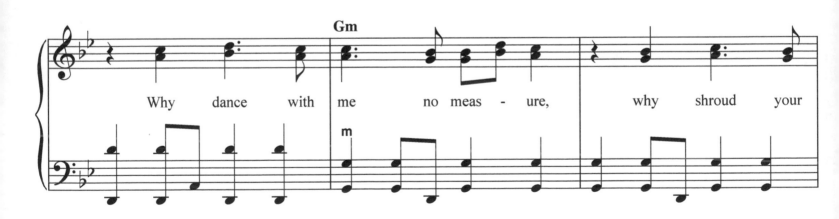

Why dance with me no meas - ure, why shroud your

D.S. al Fine
(with repeat)

beau - ty's treas - ure in mys - ter - y?

OBLIVION

By ASTOR PIAZZOLLA

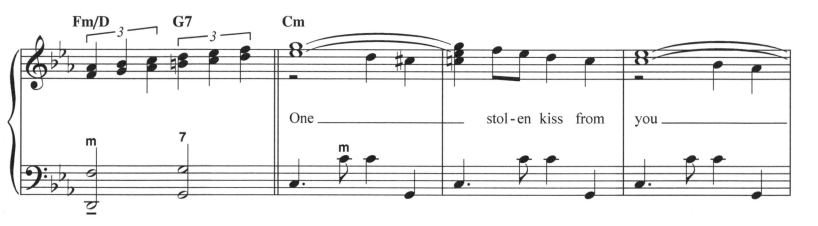

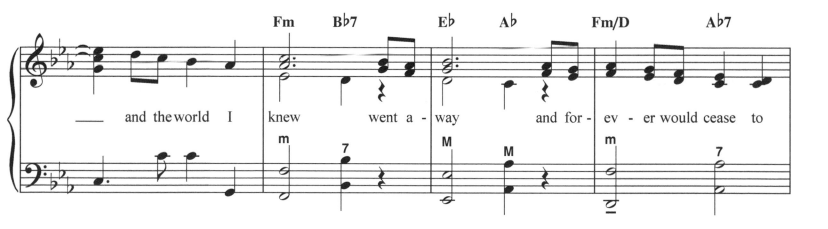

could ex-ist no more, _____ on-ly you and me. _____

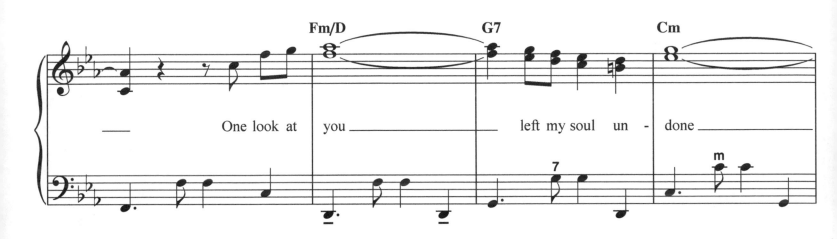

____ One look at you _____ left my soul un - done _____

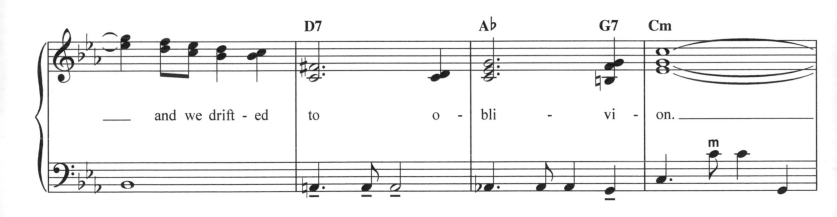

____ and we drift - ed to o - bli - vi - on. _____

____ You o - ver - come all my heart's de -

on.　　　　　　　　　　　How _____

_____ could I not have　known? _____　I am yours a - lone　　by de-

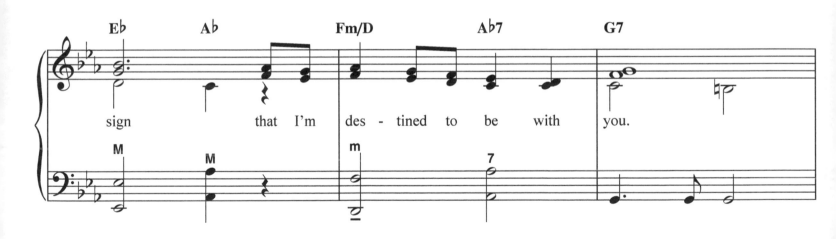

sign　　　　that I'm des - tined to be with　you.

Yours _____　for the rest　of　time _____　and the test of

time _____ we will sail right through. _____

_____ One look at you _____ left my soul un - done _____

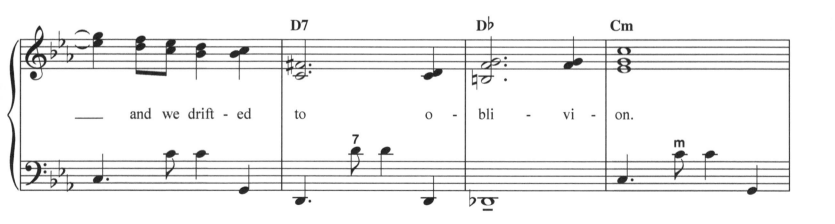

_____ and we drift - ed to o - bli - vi - on.

ORCHIDS IN THE MOONLIGHT

Words by GUS KAHN and EDWARD ELISCU
Music by VINCENT YOUMANS

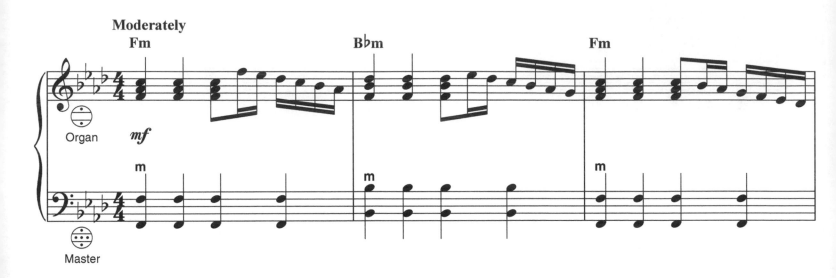

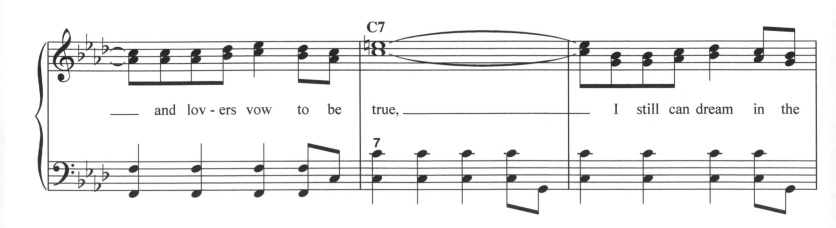

moon - light | of one dear night that we knew. _____

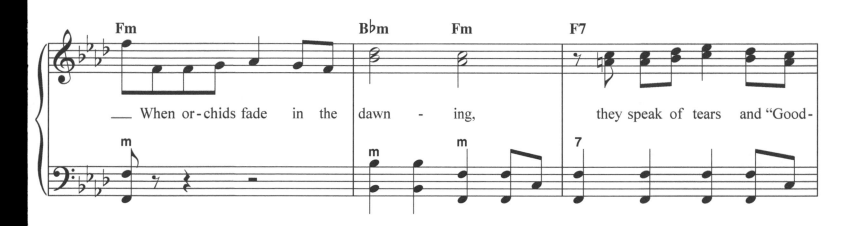

____ When or-chids fade in the dawn - ing, | they speak of tears and "Good-

bye!" _____ | Though my dreams _ are shat - tered

To Coda ⊕

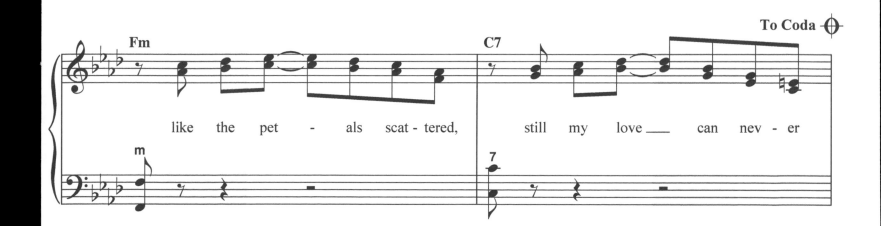

like the pet - als scat - tered, | still my love ___ can nev - er

die. There is peace in the twi - light ___

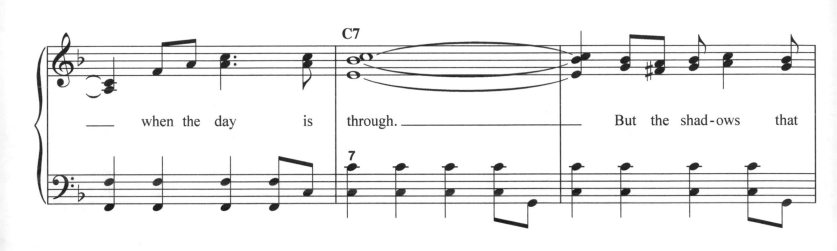

___ when the day is through. ___ But the shad-ows that

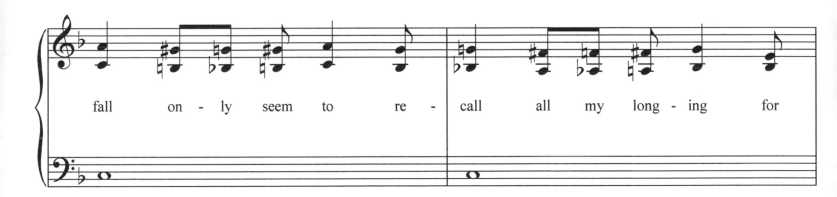

fall on - ly seem to re - call all my long-ing for

you. ___ There's a dream in the moon - beams ___

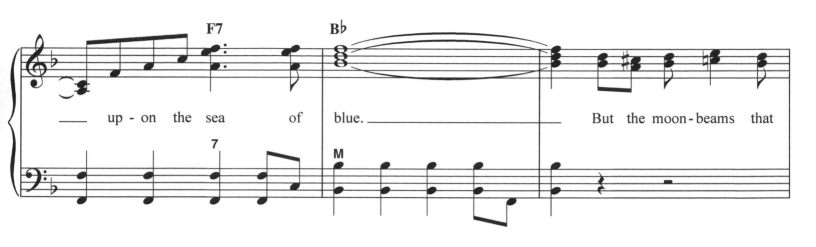

upon the sea of blue. But the moon-beams that

fall only seem to recall love is all, love is you.

D.S. al Coda

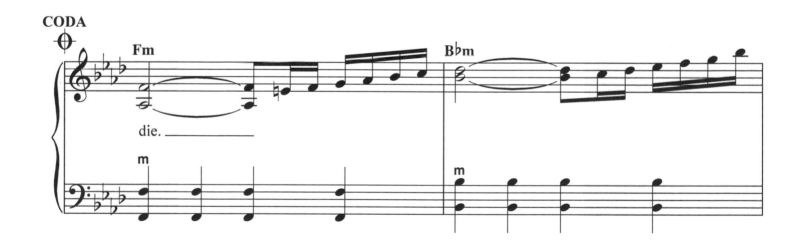

CODA

die.

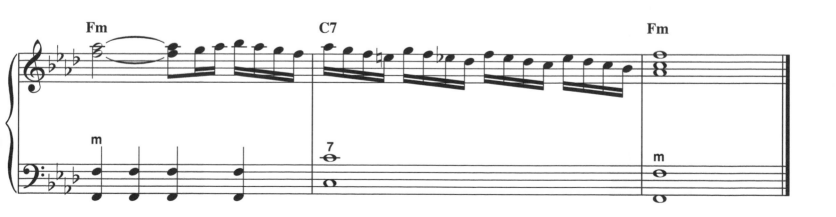

QUIZÁS, QUIZÁS, QUIZÁS
(Perhaps, Perhaps, Perhaps)

Music and Spanish Words by OSVALDO FARRES
English Words by JOE DAVIS

47

heart - ed. _____ So, if you real - ly love me, __ say
cuan - do. _____ Ya - sí pa - san los dí - as __ y

"yes," but if you don't, dear, __ con - fess and please don't
yo de - ses - pe - ra - do __ y tú, tú con - tes -

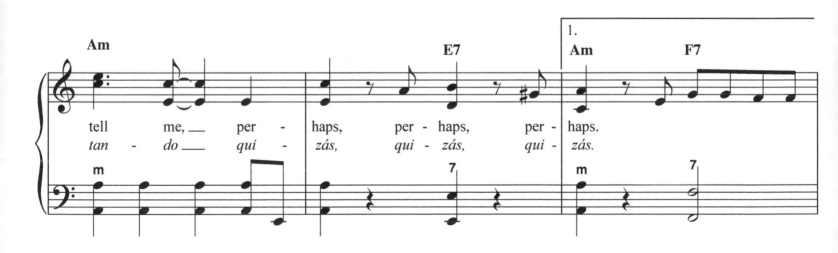

tell me, __ per - haps, per - haps, per - haps.
tan - do __ qui - zás, qui - zás, qui - zás.

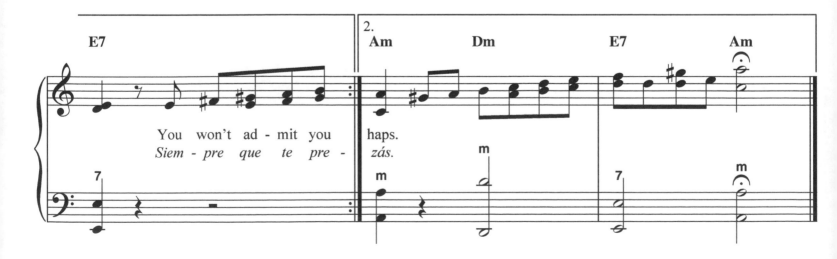

You won't ad - mit you haps.
Siem - pre que te pre - zás.

THE RAIN IN SPAIN

from MY FAIR LADY

Words by ALAN JAY LERNER
Music by FREDERICK LOEWE

rain in Spain stays main - ly in the plain. _____

Higgins: Now, once a - gain, where does it

rain? *Eliza:* On the plain! On the plain! *Higgins:* And

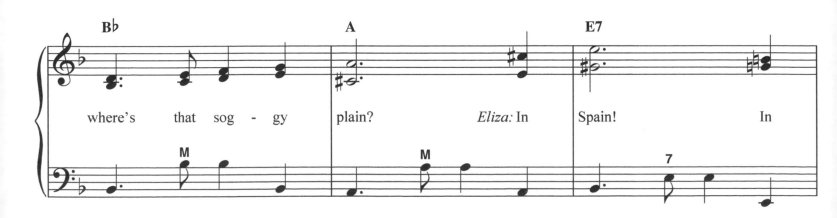

where's that sog - gy plain? *Eliza:* In Spain! In

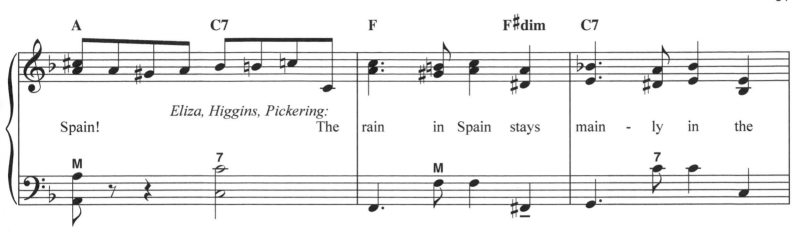

Eliza, Higgins, Pickering:

Spain!   The rain in Spain stays main - ly in the

plain. _____   The rain in Spain stays

main - ly in the   plain. _____   In

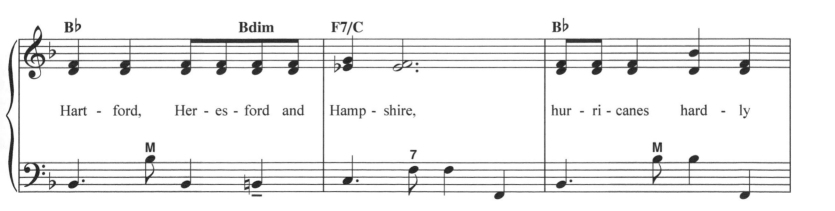

Hart - ford,   Her - es - ford and   Hamp - shire,   hur - ri - canes   hard - ly

hap - pen. How

kind of you to let me come. Now, once a - gain, where does it

rain? *Eliza:* On the plain! On the plain! *Higgins:* And

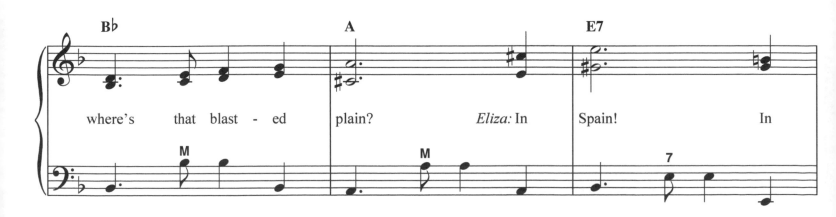

where's that blast - ed plain? *Eliza:* In Spain! In

Spain! The rain in Spain stays main - ly in the

plain. _____ The rain in Spain stays

main - ly in the plain!

WHATEVER LOLA WANTS
(Lola Gets)
from DAMN YANKEES

Words and Music by RICHARD ADLER
and JERRY ROSS

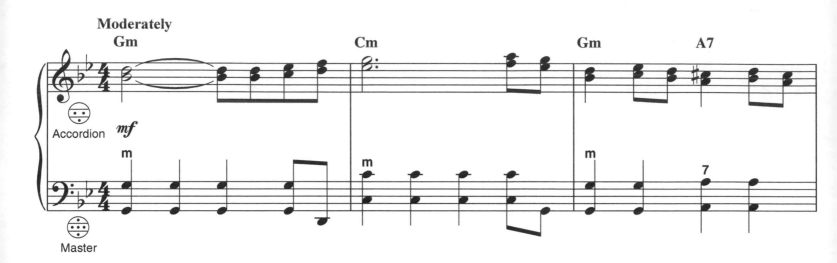

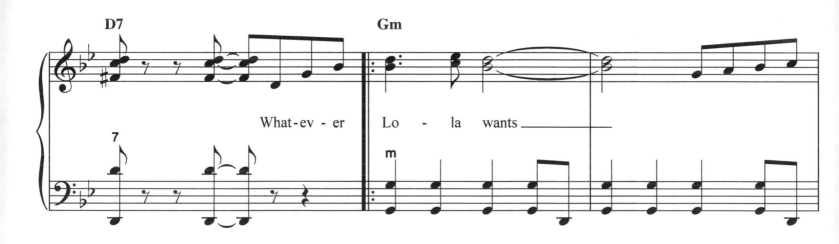

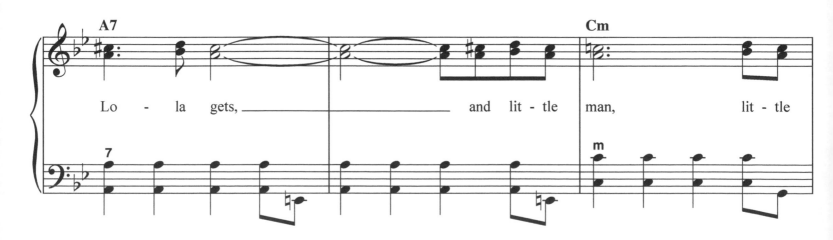

TANGO OF ROSES

Words by MARJORIE HARPER
Music by VITTORIO MASCHERONI

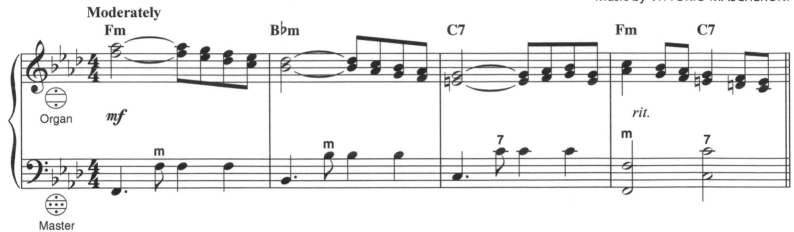

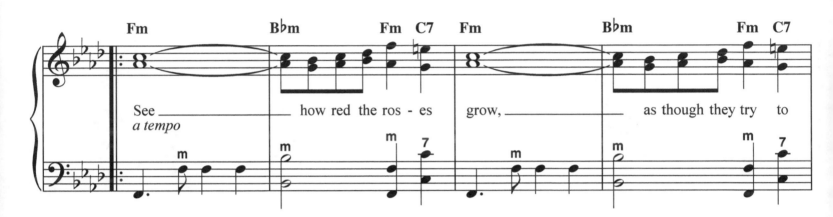

See _____ how red the ros - es grow, _____ as though they try to

show _____ the ver - y fire, _____ the same de - sire, _____ that you in-

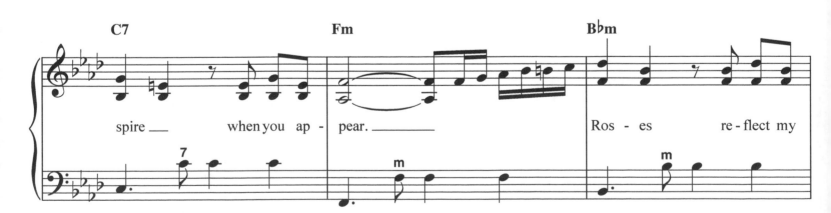

spire ___ when you ap - pear. _____ Ros - es re - flect my

gladness, they share my sadness when you're not near.

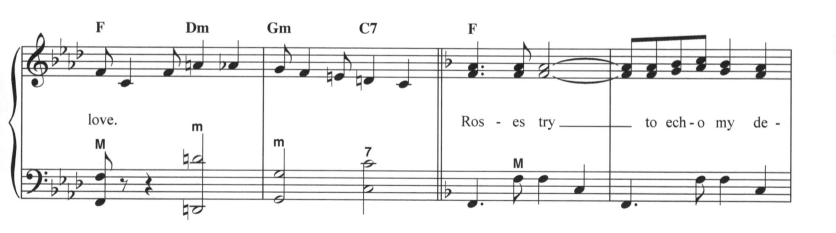

They are the emblems of passion, romance, and

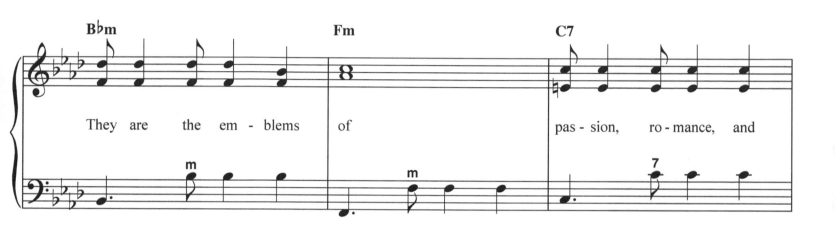

love. Roses try to echo my de-

votion. Roses seem to mirror my e-

mo - tion. _____ Yet with-in _____ the dream-y Tan - go of

Ros - es, _____ my heart so will-ing-ly dis - clos - es _____ love will out-live the

rose.

1.
Love will out-live the rose.

2.
Love will out-live the rose.

Love will out-live the rose.

HAL•LEONARD ACCORDION PLAY•ALONG

The Accordion Play-Along series features custom accordion arrangements with CD tracks recorded by a live band (accordion, bass and drums). There are two audio tracks for each song – a full performance for listening, plus a separate backing track which lets you be the soloist! The CD is playable on any CD player, and is also enhanced so Mac and PC users can adjust the recording to any tempo without changing the pitch!

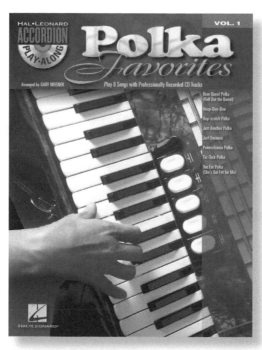

1. POLKA FAVORITES
arr. Gary Meisner

Beer Barrel Polka (Roll Out the Barrel) • Hoop-Dee-Doo • Hop-scotch Polka • Just Another Polka • Just Because • Pennsylvania Polka • Tic-Tock Polka • Too Fat Polka (She's Too Fat for Me).
00701705 Book/CD Pack.. $14.99

2. ALL-TIME HITS
arr. Gary Meisner

Edelweiss • Fly Me to the Moon (In Other Words) • I Left My Heart in San Francisco • It's a Small World • Moon River • More (Ti Guarderò Nel Cuore) • Poinciana (Song of the Tree) • When I'm Sixty-Four.
00701706 Book/CD Pack.. $14.99

3. CLASSIC SONGS
arr. Gary Meisner

Carnival of Venice • Ciribiribin • Come Back to Sorrento • Fascination (Valse Tzigane) • Funiculi, Funicula • I Love You Truly • In the Good Old Summertime • Melody of Love • Peg O' My Heart • When Irish Eyes Are Smiling.
00701707 Book/CD Pack...................................... $14.99

4. CHRISTMAS SONGS
arr. Gary Meisner

Frosty the Snow Man • Have Yourself a Merry Little Christmas • Here Comes Santa Claus (Right down Santa Claus Lane) • The Most Wonderful Time of the Year • Rudolph the Red-Nosed Reindeer • Santa Claus Is Comin' to Town • Silver Bells • Winter Wonderland.
00101770 Book/CD Pack.. $14.99

5. ITALIAN SONGS
arr. Gary Meisner

La Sorella • La Spagnola • Mattinata • 'O Sole Mio • Oh Marie • Santa Lucia • Tarantella • Vieni Sul Mar.
00101771 Book/CD Pack.. $14.99

Visit Hal Leonard online at **www.halleonard.com**

0218

A COLLECTION OF ALL-TIME FAVORITES
FOR ACCORDION

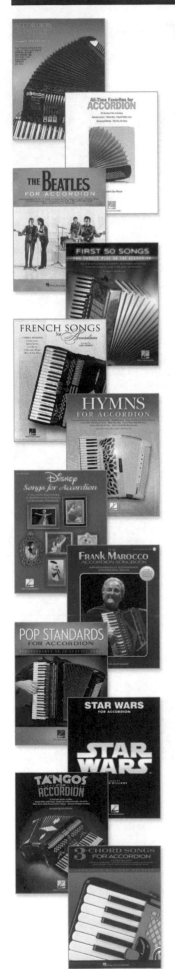

ACCORDION FAVORITES
arr. Gary Meisner

16 all-time favorites, arranged for accordion, including: Can't Smile Without You • Could I Have This Dance • Endless Love • Memory • Sunrise, Sunset • I.O.U. • and more.
00359012...$12.99

ALL-TIME FAVORITES FOR ACCORDION
arr. Gary Meisner

20 must-know standards arranged for accordions. Includes: Ain't Misbehavin' • Autumn Leaves • Crazy • Hello, Dolly! • Hey, Good Lookin' • Moon River • Speak Softly, Love • Unchained Melody • The Way We Were • Zip-A-Dee-Doo-Dah • and more.
00311088...$12.99

THE BEATLES FOR ACCORDION

17 hits from the Lads from Liverpool have been arranged for accordion. Includes: All You Need Is Love • Eleanor Rigby • The Fool on the Hill • Here Comes the Sun • Hey Jude • In My Life • Let It Be • Ob-La-Di, Ob-La-Da • Penny Lane • When I'm Sixty-Four • Yesterday • and more.
00268724 ....$14.99

BROADWAY FAVORITES
arr. Ken Kotwitz

A collection of 17 wonderful show songs, including: Don't Cry for Me Argentina • Getting to Know You • If I Were a Rich Man • Oklahoma • People Will Say We're in Love • We Kiss in a Shadow.
00490157...$10.99

DISNEY SONGS FOR ACCORDION – 3RD EDITION

13 Disney favorites especially arranged for accordion, including: Be Our Guest • Beauty and the Beast • Can You Feel the Love Tonight • Chim Chim Cher-ee • It's a Small World • Let It Go • Under the Sea • A Whole New World • You'll Be in My Heart • Zip-A-Dee-Doo-Dah • and more!
00152508 ....$12.99

FIRST 50 SONGS YOU SHOULD PLAY ON THE ACCORDION
arr. Gary Meisner

If you're new to the accordion, you are probably eager to learn some songs. This book provides 50 simplified arrangements of must-know popular standards, folk songs and show tunes, including: All of Me • Beer Barrel Polka • Carnival of Venice • Edelweiss • Hava Nagila (Let's Be Happy) • Hernando's Hideaway • Jambalaya (On the Bayou) • Lady of Spain • Moon River • 'O Sole Mio • Sentimental Journey • Somewhere, My Love • That's Amore (That's Love) • Under Paris Skies • and more. Includes lyrics when applicable.
00250269 ....$16.99

FRENCH SONGS FOR ACCORDION
arr. Gary Meisner

A très magnifique collection of 17 French standards arranged for the accordion. Includes: Autumn Leaves • Beyond the Sea • C'est Magnifique • I Love Paris • La Marseillaise • Let It Be Me (Je T'appartiens) • Under Paris Skies • Watch What Happens • and more.
00311498...$10.99

HYMNS FOR ACCORDION
arr. Gary Meisner

24 treasured sacred favorites arranged for accordion, including: Amazing Grace • Beautiful Savior • Come, Thou Fount of Every Blessing • Crown Him with Many Crowns • Holy, Holy, Holy • It Is Well with My Soul • Just a Closer Walk with Thee • A Mighty Fortress Is Our God • Nearer, My God, to Thee • The Old Rugged Cross • Rock of Ages • What a Friend We Have in Jesus • and more.
00277160 ....$9.99

ITALIAN SONGS FOR ACCORDION
arr. Gary Meisner

17 favorite Italian standards arranged for accordion, including: Carnival of Venice • Ciribiribin • Come Back to Sorrento • Funiculi, Funicula • La donna è mobile • La Spagnola • 'O Sole Mio • Santa Lucia • Tarantella • and more.
00311089...$9.95

LATIN FAVORITES FOR ACCORDION
arr. Gary Meisner

20 Latin favorites, including: Bésame Mucho (Kiss Me Much) • The Girl from Ipanema • How Insensitive (Insensatez) • Perfidia • Spanish Eyes • So Nice (Summer Samba) • and more.
00310932...$14.99

THE FRANK MAROCCO ACCORDION SONGBOOK

This songbook includes arrangements and recordings of 15 standards and original songs from legendary jazz accordionist Frank Marocco, including: All the Things You Are • Autumn Leaves • Beyond the Sea • Moon River • Moonlight in Vermont • Stormy Weather (Keeps Rainin' All the Time) • and more!
00233441 Book/Online Audio...............$19.99

POP STANDARDS FOR ACCORDION
Arrangements of 20 Classic Songs

20 classic pop standards arranged for accordion are included in this collection: Annie's Song • Chances Are • For Once in My Life • Help Me Make It Through the Night • My Cherie Amour • Ramblin' Rose • (Sittin' On) The Dock of the Bay • That's Amore (That's Love) • Unchained Melody • and more.
00254822 ....$14.99

POLKA FAVORITES
arr. Kenny Kotwitz

An exciting new collection of 16 songs, including: Beer Barrel Polka • Liechtensteiner Polka • My Melody of Love • Paloma Blanca • Pennsylvania Polka • Too Fat Polka • and more.
00311573...$12.99

STAR WARS FOR ACCORDION

A dozen songs from the Star Wars franchise: The Imperial March (Darth Vader's Theme) • Luke and Leia • March of the Resistance • Princess Leia's Theme • Rey's Theme • Star Wars (Main Theme) • and more.
00157380 ....$14.99

TANGOS FOR ACCORDION
arr. Gary Meisner

Every accordionist needs to know some tangos! Here are 15 favorites: Amapola (Pretty Little Poppy) • Aquellos Ojos Verdes (Green Eyes) • Hernando's Hideaway • Jalousie (Jealousy) • Kiss of Fire • La Cumparsita (The Masked One) • Quizás, Quizás, Quizás (Perhaps, Perhaps, Perhaps) • The Rain in Spain • Tango of Roses • Whatever Lola Wants (Lola Gets) • and more!
00122252 ....$9.99

3-CHORD SONGS FOR ACCORDION
arr. Gary Meisner

Here are nearly 30 songs that are easy to play but still sound great! Includes: Amazing Grace • Can Can • Danny Boy • For He's a Jolly Good Fellow • He's Got the Whole World in His Hands • Just a Closer Walk with Thee • La Paloma Blanca (The White Dove) • My Country, 'Tis of Thee • Ode to Joy • Oh! Susanna • Yankee Doodle • The Yellow Rose of Texas • and more.
00312104 ....$12.99

LAWRENCE WELK'S POLKA FOLIO

More than 50 famous polkas, schottisches and waltzes arranged for piano and accordion, including: Blue Eyes • Budweiser Polka • Clarinet Polka • Cuckoo Polka • The Dove Polka • Draw One Polka • Gypsy Polka • Helena Polka • International Waltzes • Let's Have Another One • Schnitzelbank • Shuffle Schottische • Squeeze Box Polka • Waldteuful Waltzes • and more.
00123218...$12.99

HAL•LEONARD®
Visit Hal Leonard Online at
www.halleonard.com

The Best-Selling Jazz Book of All Time Is Now Legal!

The Real Books are the most popular jazz books of all time. Since the 1970s, musicians have trusted these volumes to get them through every gig, night after night. The problem is that the books were illegally produced and distributed, without any regard to copyright law, or royalties paid to the composers who created these musical masterpieces.

Hal Leonard is very proud to present the first legitimate and legal editions of these books ever produced. You won't even notice the difference, other than all the notorious errors being fixed: the covers and typeface look the same, the song lists are nearly identical, and the price for our edition is even cheaper than the originals!

Every conscientious musician will appreciate that these books are now produced accurately and ethically, benefitting the songwriters that we owe for some of the greatest tunes of all time!

VOLUME 1

00240221	C Edition	$39.99
00240224	B♭ Edition	$39.99
00240225	E♭ Edition	$39.99
00240226	Bass Clef Edition	$39.99
00286389	F Edition	$39.99
00240292	C Edition 6 x 9	$35.00
00240339	B♭ Edition 6 x 9	$35.00
00147792	Bass Clef Edition 6 x 9	$35.00
00451087	C Edition on CD-ROM	$29.99
00200984	Online Backing Tracks: Selections	$45.00
00110604	Book/USB Flash Drive Backing Tracks Pack	$79.99
00110599	USB Flash Drive Only	$50.00

VOLUME 2

00240222	C Edition	$39.99
00240227	B♭ Edition	$39.99
00240228	E♭ Edition	$39.99
00240229	Bass Clef Edition	$39.99
00240293	C Edition 6 x 9	$35.00
00125900	B♭ Edition 6 x 9	$35.00
00451088	C Edition on CD-ROM	$30.99
00125900	The Real Book – Mini Edition	$35.00
00204126	Backing Tracks on USB Flash Drive	$50.00
00204131	C Edition – USB Flash Drive Pack	$79.99

VOLUME 3

00240233	C Edition	$39.99
00240284	B♭ Edition	$39.99
00240285	E♭ Edition	$39.99
00240286	Bass Clef Edition	$39.99
00240338	C Edition 6 x 9	$35.00
00451089	C Edition on CD-ROM	$29.99

VOLUME 4

00240296	C Edition	$39.99
00103348	B♭ Edition	$39.99
00103349	E♭ Edition	$39.99
00103350	Bass Clef Edition	$39.99

VOLUME 5

00240349	C Edition	$39.99
00175278	B♭ Edition	$39.99
00175279	E♭ Edition	$39.99

VOLUME 6

00240534	C Edition	$39.99
00223637	E♭ Edition	$39.99

Also available:

00154230	The Real Bebop Book	$34.99
00240264	The Real Blues Book	$34.99
00310910	The Real Bluegrass Book	$35.00
00240223	The Real Broadway Book	$35.00
00240440	The Trane Book	$22.99
00125426	The Real Country Book	$39.99
00269721	The Real Miles Davis Book C Edition	$24.99
00269723	The Real Miles Davis Book B♭ Edition	$24.99
00240355	The Real Dixieland Book C Edition	$32.50
00294853	The Real Dixieland Book E♭ Edition	$35.00
00122335	The Real Dixieland Book B♭ Edition	$35.00
00240235	The Duke Ellington Real Book	$22.99
00240268	The Real Jazz Solos Book	$30.00
00240348	The Real Latin Book C Edition	$37.50
00127107	The Real Latin Book B♭ Edition	$35.00
00120809	The Pat Metheny Real Book C Edition	$27.50
00252119	The Pat Metheny Real Book B♭ Edition	$24.99
00240358	The Charlie Parker Real Book C Edition	$19.99
00275997	The Charlie Parker Real Book E♭ Edition	$19.99
00118324	The Real Pop Book – Vol. 1	$35.00
00240331	The Bud Powell Real Book	$19.99
00240437	The Real R&B Book C Edition	$39.99
00276590	The Real R&B Book B♭ Edition	$39.99
00240313	The Real Rock Book	$35.00
00240323	The Real Rock Book – Vol. 2	$35.00
00240359	The Real Tab Book	$32.50
00240317	The Real Worship Book	$29.99

THE REAL CHRISTMAS BOOK

00240306	C Edition	$32.50
00240345	B♭ Edition	$32.50
00240346	E♭ Edition	$35.00
00240347	Bass Clef Edition	$32.50
00240431	A-G CD Backing Tracks	$24.99
00240432	H-M CD Backing Tracks	$24.99
00240433	N-Y CD Backing Tracks	$24.99

THE REAL VOCAL BOOK

00240230	Volume 1 High Voice	$35.00
00240307	Volume 1 Low Voice	$35.00
00240231	Volume 2 High Voice	$35.00
00240308	Volume 2 Low Voice	$35.00
00240391	Volume 3 High Voice	$35.00
00240392	Volume 3 Low Voice	$35.00
00118318	Volume 4 High Voice	$35.00
00118319	Volume 4 Low Voice	$35.00

Complete song lists online at www.halleonard.com

Prices, content, and availability subject to change without notice.

0719
318

THE ULTIMATE COLLECTION OF
FAKE BOOKS

The Real Book – Sixth Edition

Hal Leonard proudly presents the first legitimate and legal editions of these books ever produced. These bestselling titles are mandatory for anyone who plays jazz! Over 400 songs, including: All By Myself • Dream a Little Dream of Me • God Bless the Child • Like Someone in Love • When I Fall in Love • and more.

00240221 Volume 1, C Instruments $45.00
00240224 Volume 1, B♭ Instruments $45.00
00240225 Volume 1, E♭ Instruments $45.00
00240226 Volume 1, BC Instruments $45.00

**Go to halleonard.com
to view all *Real Books* available**

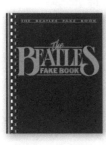

The Beatles Fake Book

200 of the Beatles' hits: All You Need Is Love • Blackbird • Can't Buy Me Love • Day Tripper • Eleanor Rigby • The Fool on the Hill • Hey Jude • In My Life • Let It Be • Michelle • Norwegian Wood (This Bird Has Flown) • Penny Lane • Revolution • She Loves You • Twist and Shout • With a Little Help from My Friends • Yesterday • and many more!
00240069 C Instruments $39.99

The Best Fake Book Ever

More than 1,000 songs from all styles of music: All My Loving • At the Hop • Cabaret • Dust in the Wind • Fever • Hello, Dolly • Hey Jude • King of the Road • Longer • Misty • Route 66 • Sentimental Journey • Somebody • Song Sung Blue • Spinning Wheel • Unchained Melody • We Will Rock You • What a Wonderful World • Wooly Bully • Y.M.C.A. • and more.

00290239 C Instruments $49.99
00240084 E♭ Instruments $49.95

The Celtic Fake Book

Over 400 songs from Ireland, Scotland and Wales: Auld Lang Syne • Barbara Allen • Danny Boy • Finnegan's Wake • The Galway Piper • Irish Rover • Loch Lomond • Molly Malone • My Bonnie Lies Over the Ocean • My Wild Irish Rose • That's an Irish Lullaby • and more. Includes Gaelic lyrics where applicable and a pronunciation guide.
00240153 C Instruments $25.00

Classic Rock Fake Book

Over 250 of the best rock songs of all time: American Woman • Beast of Burden • Carry On Wayward Son • Dream On • Free Ride • Hurts So Good • I Shot the Sheriff • Layla • My Generation • Nights in White Satin • Owner of a Lonely Heart • Rhiannon • Roxanne • Summer of '69 • We Will Rock You • You Ain't Seen Nothin' Yet • and lots more!

00240108 C Instruments $35.00

Classical Fake Book

This unprecedented, amazingly comprehensive reference includes over 850 classical themes and melodies for all classical music lovers. Includes everything from Renaissance music to Vivaldi and Mozart to Mendelssohn. Lyrics in the original language are included when appropriate.
00240044 ....$39.99

The Disney Fake Book

Even more Disney favorites, including: The Bare Necessities • Can You Feel the Love Tonight • Circle of Life • How Do You Know? • Let It Go • Part of Your World • Reflection • Some Day My Prince Will Come • When I See an Elephant Fly • You'll Be in My Heart • and many more.
00175311 C Instruments $34.99
Disney characters & artwork TM & © 2021 Disney

The Folksong Fake Book

Over 1,000 folksongs: Bury Me Not on the Lone Prairie • Clementine • The Erie Canal • Go, Tell It on the Mountain • Home on the Range • Kumbaya • Michael Row the Boat Ashore • Shenandoah • Simple Gifts • Swing Low, Sweet Chariot • When Johnny Comes Marching Home • Yankee Doodle • and many more.
00240151 ....$34.99

The Hal Leonard Real Jazz Standards Fake Book

Over 250 standards in easy-to-read authentic hand-written jazz engravings: Ain't Misbehavin' • Blue Skies • Crazy He Calls Me • Desafinado (Off Key) • Fever • How High the Moon • It Don't Mean a Thing (If It Ain't Got That Swing) • Lazy River • Mood Indigo • Old Devil Moon • Route 66 • Satin Doll • Witchcraft • and more.
00240161 C Instruments $45.00

The Hymn Fake Book

Nearly 1,000 multi-denominational hymns perfect for church musicians or hobbyists: Amazing Grace • Christ the Lord Is Risen Today • For the Beauty of the Earth • It Is Well with My Soul • A Mighty Fortress Is Our God • O for a Thousand Tongues to Sing • Praise to the Lord, the Almighty • Take My Life and Let It Be • What a Friend We Have in Jesus • and hundreds more!
00240145 C Instruments $29.99

The New Broadway Fake Book

This amazing collection includes 645 songs from 285 shows: All I Ask of You • Any Dream Will Do • Close Every Door • Consider Yourself • Dancing Queen • Mack the Knife • Mamma Mia • Memory • The Phantom of the Opera • Popular • Strike up the Band • and more!
00138905 C Instruments $45.00

The Praise & Worship Fake Book

Over 400 songs including: Amazing Grace (My Chains Are Gone) • Cornerstone • Everlasting God • Great Are You Lord • In Christ Alone • Mighty to Save • Open the Eyes of My Heart • Shine, Jesus, Shine • This Is Amazing Grace • and more.
00160838 C Instruments $39.99
00240324 B♭ Instruments $34.99

Three Chord Songs Fake Book

200 classic and contemporary 3-chord tunes in melody/lyric/chord format: Ain't No Sunshine • Bang a Gong (Get It On) • Cold, Cold Heart • Don't Worry, Be Happy • Give Me One Reason • I Got You (I Feel Good) • Kiss • Me and Bobby McGee • Rock This Town • Werewolves of London • You Don't Mess Around with Jim • and more.
00240387 ....$34.99

The Ultimate Christmas Fake Book

The 6th edition of this bestseller features over 270 traditional and contemporary Christmas hits: Have Yourself a Merry Little Christmas • I'll Be Home for Christmas O Come, All Ye Faithful (Adeste Fideles) • Santa Baby • Winter Wonderland • and more.
00147215 C Instruments $30.00

The Ultimate Country Fake Book

This book includes over 700 of your favorite country hits: Always on My Mind • Boot Scootin' Boogie • Crazy • Down at the Twist and Shout • Forever and Ever, Amen • Friends in Low Places • The Gambler • Jambalaya • King of the Road • Sixteen Tons • There's a Tear in My Beer • Your Cheatin' Heart • and hundreds more.
00240049 C Instruments $49.99

The Ultimate Fake Book

Includes over 1,200 hits: Blue Skies • Body and Soul • Endless Love • Isn't It Romantic? • Memory • Mona Lisa • Moon River • Operator • Piano Man • Roxanne • Satin Doll • Shout • Small World • Smile • Speak Softly, Love • Strawberry Fields Forever • Tears in Heaven • Unforgettable • hundreds more!
00240024 C Instruments $55.00
00240026 B♭ Instruments $49.95

The Ultimate Jazz Fake Book

This must-own collection includes 635 songs spanning all jazz styles from more than 9 decades. Songs include: Maple Leaf Rag • Basin Street Blues • A Night in Tunisia • Lullaby of Birdland • The Girl from Ipanema • Bag's Groove • I Can't Get Started • All the Things You Are • and many more!
00240079 C Instruments $45.00
00240080 B♭ Instruments $45.00
00240081 E♭ Instruments $45.00

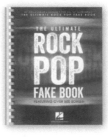

The Ultimate Rock Pop Fake Book

This amazing collection features nearly 550 rock and pop hits: American Pie • Bohemian Rhapsody • Born to Be Wild • Clocks • Dancing with Myself • Eye of the Tiger • Proud Mary • Rocket Man • Should I Stay or Should I Go • Total Eclipse of the Heart • Unchained Melody • When Doves Cry • Y.M.C.A. • You Raise Me Up • and more.
00240310 C Instruments $39.99

**Complete songlists available online at
www.halleonard.com**

HAL•LEONARD®